W9-BWH-479

DISCARD

Getting
Started With
Math

Using Math Outdoors

By Amy Rauen

Illustrations by Lorin Walter

Reading consultant: Susan Nations, M.Ed.,
author/literacy coach/consultant in literacy development

Math consultant: Rhea Stewart, M.A., mathematics content specialist

WEEKLY READER®
PUBLISHING

Please visit our web site at www.garethstevens.com
For a free color catalog describing our list of high-quality books,
call 1-800-542-2595 (USA) or 1-800-387-3178 (Canada). Our fax: 1-877-542-2596

Library of Congress Cataloging-in-Publication Data

Rauen, Amy.
    Using math outdoors / Amy Rauen.
        p. cm. — (Getting started with math)
    ISBN-13: 978-0-8368-8984-0 (lib. bdg.)
    ISBN-10: 0-8368-8984-3 (lib. bdg.)
    ISBN-13: 978-0-8368-8989-5 (softcover)
    ISBN-10: 0-8368-8989-4 (softcover)
    1. Counting—Juvenile literature.   I. Title.
    QA113.R379   2008
    513—dc22   2007026333

This edition first published in 2008 by
Weekly Reader® Books
An Imprint of Gareth Stevens Publishing
1 Reader's Digest Road
Pleasantville, NY 10570-7000 USA

Copyright © 2008 by Gareth Stevens, Inc.

Senior Editor: Brian Fitzgerald
Creative Director: Lisa Donovan
Graphic Designer: Alexandria Davis

Printed in the United States of America

1 2 3 4 5 6 7 8 9 10 09 08 07

Note to Educators and Parents

Reading is such an exciting adventure for young children! They are beginning to match the spoken word to print and learn directionality and print conventions, among other skills. Books that are appropriate for emergent readers incorporate these conventions while also informing and entertaining them.

The books in the *Getting Started With Math* series are designed to support young readers in the earliest stages of literacy. Readers will love looking at the full-color photographs and illustrations as they develop skills in early math concepts. This integration allows young children to maximize their learning as they see how thoughts and ideas connect across content areas.

In addition to serving as wonderful picture books in schools, libraries, and homes, the *Getting Started With Math* books are specifically intended to be read within guided small reading groups. The small group setting enables the teacher or other adult to provide scaffolding that will boost the reader's effort. Children and adults alike will find these books supportive, engaging, and fun!

Susan Nations, M.Ed.
author/literacy coach/consultant in literacy development

It is summer!
I visit the beach.

I can do math at the beach.
I count many things.

I count 8 big umbrellas.

I count 15 birds.

They fly in the sky over the sea.

I see 10 rocks and 5 shells.
There are more rocks than shells.

I see 3 shovels and 7 pails.
There are fewer shovels than pails.

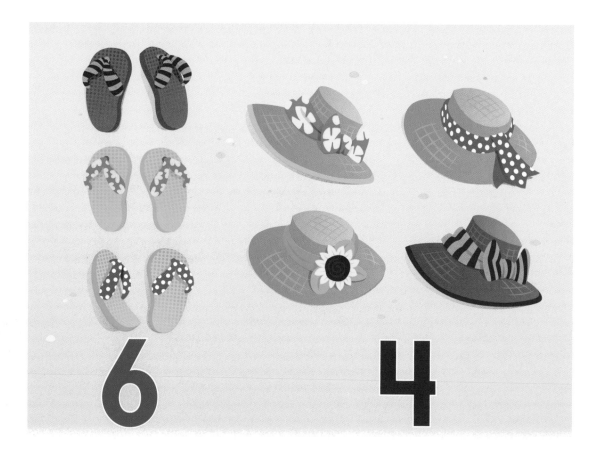

I see 6 sandals and 4 hats.

There are more sandals than hats.

I see 2 big birds. I see 2 small birds.
I see 4 birds in all.

I see 1 green pail. I see 4 blue pails.
I see 5 pails in all.

Math at the beach is fun!

Glossary

bird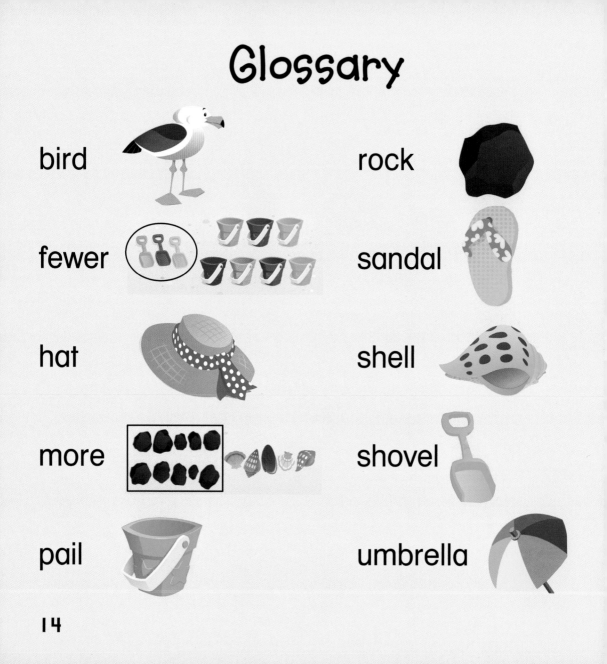

fewer

hat

more

pail

rock

sandal

shell

shovel

umbrella

Show What You Know

1. How many letters are in each of these words?

   hat   **shell**   **umbrella**

2. Which group has more?

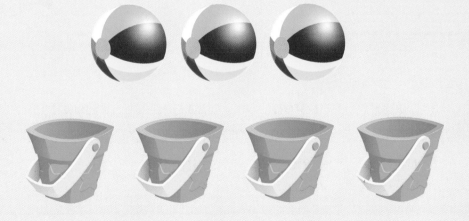

To Find Out More

Just Enough Carrots. Mathstart (series).
Stuart J. Murphy (HarperCollins Children's Books)

More, Fewer, Less.
Tana Hoban (Greenwillow Press)

About the Author

Amy Rauen is the author of more than a dozen math books for children. She also designs and writes educational software. Amy lives in San Diego, California, with her husband and their two cats.